Table Style

Table Style

101 creative ideas for elegant and affordable entertaining

Liz Belton
& Rebecca Tanqueray

Photography by Debi Treloar

RYLAND
PETERS
& SMALL
LONDON NEW YORK

Styling Liz Belton
Text Rebecca Tanqueray

Senior designer Megan Smith
Commissioning editor Annabel Morgan
Location research Jess Walton
Production Gordana Simakovic
Art director Leslie Harrington
Publishing director Alison Starling

First published in 2010 by
Ryland Peters and Small
20–21 Jockey's Fields
London WC1R 4BW
and
519 Broadway, 5th Floor
New York, NY 10012

www.rylandpeters.com

10 9 8 7 6 5 4 3 2

Text © Ryland Peters & Small 2010
Design and photographs
© Ryland Peters & Small 2010

ISBN: 978-1-84597-967-6

A CIP record for this book is
available from the British Library.

Printed and bound in China

Library of Congress Cataloging-in-
Publication Data

Belton, Liz.
  Table style : elegant & affordable ideas for
decorating the table / Liz Belton & Rebecca
Tanqueray ; photography by Debi Treloar. --
1st ed.
    p. cm.
  Includes index.
  ISBN 978-1-84597-967-6
  1. Table setting and decoration. I.
Tanqueray, Rebecca. II. Treloar,
Debi. III. Title.
  TX879.B45 2010
  642'.6--dc22

2009047648

contents

introduction

Table setting used to be a very formal affair, with strict rules and regulations for every occasion. Tableware reflected status, and thus presenting it correctly was a key social skill. Today, entertaining has become far more relaxed and laissez faire, and we have happily abandoned all that pomp and circumstance. But along the way, it seems we have lost something else, too – the art of creating a beautiful table.

Setting the table for lunch with friends or a celebratory family dinner shouldn't be a chore or an afterthought. Creating a decorative tabletop is easy, satisfying and fun, and even the simplest scheme will have a transforming effect on the atmosphere of any occasion – and on your guests. *Table Style* is packed with ideas to inspire you, whether you're throwing a baby shower, having a cocktail party or celebrating Mother's Day. The settings are easy to achieve without requiring a new cupboard of dinnerware. Successful table dressing is not about silver spoons or fine crystal; it's about making the most of what you have.

The first section, The Elements, explains how to build a core collection of versatile pieces that will allow you to create any number of fabulous settings. The Occasions contains a multitude of stylish ideas for everything from a weekend brunch to a formal dinner. And finally, at the back of the book, there's a brief guide to international place settings that will prove a useful reference.

the elements

Repositories of hand-me-downs, holiday buys and
high-street basics, our cupboards hold more potential
than we think. Rummage through and reassess your
tableware — with just a few additions, you'll have all
the elements for a show-stopping tabletop.

dinnerware

It wasn't all that long ago that owning a smart dinner service was essential. Saved up for piece by piece or given as a present, this staple of the wedding list was a treasured possession, only brought out on special occasions.

Today, entertaining is a much more informal affair, and keeping fine china 'just for best' seems a wasteful concept. Now that we are far more likely to have friends round for a relaxed kitchen supper than to serve a formal dinner in the dining room, we need dinnerware we can use whatever the occasion.

If you are starting a collection from scratch, you don't need to spend a huge amount of money. Choose a good basic service that you can use every day and dress up for parties; a simple design or plain colour will give you most flexibility when it comes to dressing the table.

all white (opposite) Plain white china is hard to beat. Not only does it set food off perfectly but it goes with everything else on the table, too. Add pattern and texture in placemats, coasters or tablecloths to make the setting more visually interesting. do-it-all dishes (above left) Bowls can be used for serving everything from cereal to soup, pasta and pudding, so it's sensible to have a variety of sizes. Mix plain and patterned designs to make a pretty place setting. charger plates (above centre) A smart alternative to a placemat, chargers (or underplates) bring grandeur to the tabletop and can also add colour or pattern. Choose a tone that complements the china and the cloth to bring the look together. mid-century modern (above right) 1950s designs are popular and practical. Hunt them out in second-hand stores or on the internet.

dainty dishes (right) Decorative vintage plates are perfect for puddings or for teatime. Hunt around in antiques markets for those with fluted edges or floral patterns, and use a mixture of both to create an appealing old-fashioned tabletop.

storage space (below) To keep your china in mint condition, store it carefully and make sure that everyday dinnerware is easy to access. Shelves of varying depth, such as the ones here, are very useful, giving separate space for glasses, bowls and dinnerware.

Invest in as many settings as you require (a standard service for eight is a good starting point) and think about which pieces you really need. Would you prefer individual cereal, soup and pudding bowls, or one dish that does it all? Will you get more use from capacious pasta bowls or streamlined dinner plates? If a matching set is a priority, check that your chosen china is a stock item so that broken pieces will be easily replaceable.

Today, there are many styles of dinnerware available, from rustic earthenware to modern melamine to delicate vintage china, and most of us end up with a combination of different pieces. As a rule of thumb, try to match the dinnerware to the occasion and to the food you are serving; delicate puddings, for example, call for dainty plates. The advantage of choosing a plain white set of china is that it will go with everything. But patterned services or even a completely mismatched collection can work just as well, too, and will make also your tabletop more personal and interesting.

If you want to add to your china cupboard, you'll be spoilt for choice. Homeware stores on the high street and the internet stock a vast array of modern designs; antiques shops and auction houses are both good sources of inexpensive vintage pieces. What you end up with will depend largely on your taste and your budget, of course, but don't forget to consider the practicalities. Do you have storage space for that stack of chunky bamboo bowls, and will you mind handwashing those pretty retro plates?

mugs' game (above) If you don't want to handwash china, make sure any new pieces are dishwasher-safe before you buy.

less is more (left) An all-white table can be dressy. Here, a self-patterned plate on embossed wallpaper creates a chic setting.

pretty practical (left) Every tabletop requires a set of water glasses, but they needn't be purely functional. These pretty etched glasses, with their Japanese-inspired design, bring colour and subtle pattern to the table.

lacy detail (below) Decorative glassware adds an extra dimension to a tabletop, particularly if it highlights or continues a theme. These dainty transfer-printed tumblers, for example, pick up on the lace of the antique cloth beneath and would look good both on a vintage-style or contemporary table.

pretty mix (opposite) Invest in a wide selection of drinkware – from vintage wine goblets to cute and colourful, hand-decorated tumblers – so that you can mix and match different shapes and styles on the tabletop to suit every occasion.

glassware

Pretty glasses can be the making of a dinner table, adding sparkle and height to an otherwise flat array of tableware. Today, there are many styles available, from utilitarian tumblers to dainty flutes and etched cocktail glasses and, while any drinking glass should, above all, be functional, it can also add a lovely decorative element to your tabletop.

It's a good idea to start off with a basic collection of glasses that includes a variety of shapes and sizes, giving you the flexibility to cater for several different occasions. While you might make do with a simple tumbler or wine

glass for everyday meals, you may want a wider selection when you have friends for supper or serve both red and white wine for a special lunch or dinner. It's sensible to start off with a mixed collection of good-quality glasses that works for you; you can always supplement it with the odd vintage piece or junk-shop find at a later date. Adding just a few pieces of ornate or unusual glassware to the table – a pretty antique jug, perhaps, a modern carafe or some jewel-coloured water glasses – brings an extra decorative element to any scheme.

Drinking glasses can also be used as inspired 'dishes' for delicate puddings. A slender-stemmed cocktail glass or champagne coupe can be perfect for serving a sweet Muscat jelly or sharp lemon syllabub, while little shot glasses are just the right size for a rich chocolate mousse. You might also want to use pieces of glassware to display flowers on the tabletop. A row of tiny tumblers filled with grasses and blossoms can make a lovely focal point, and even a single perfect bloom popped in a liqueur glass will bring a table to life.

fine design (above) Any glass should be a pleasure to drink from, so buy the best you can afford. Thin clear glass or crystal is considered top of the range.

pretty pitchers (opposite) A jug of water is essential on any table. Choose a decorative design to make it special.

flower glass (right) Chunky rounded tumblers work brilliantly on a modern tabletop, whether you are drinking whisky or wine. They are hard to knock over, they fit in the dishwasher and you can even use them for displaying flowers.

table wine (below) A decanter or carafe of wine on a tabletop can look more elegant than a bottle and decanting a stronger red wine will give it a chance to 'breathe'. Some designs even have a chilling insert to keep white wine cold.

While it is tempting to choose pieces on the basis of looks alone, it's worth remembering that the design of a glass can affect the taste of what you are drinking. Sipping water from a chunky ceramic mug, for example, just doesn't feel right, while a beer glass will do nothing to enhance the flavours of an expensive wine. Try to provide suitable glasses for whatever drinks you are serving.

One last thing to think about before you splash out on that set of vintage 1930s cocktail glasses is the washing-up. Most antique glassware should not be washed in the dishwasher and even good modern pieces can go cloudy over time or are easily broken. Expensive glassware should be washed by hand and the dishwasher reserved for everyday items that are easily and cheaply replaced.

cutlery/flatware

Given that the knife, fork and spoon are simply tools for eating, it is remarkable quite how many different designs you can find today. Cutlery/flatware comes in all kinds of materials – silver, stainless steel, plastic, bone, wood, bamboo – and a wide variety of styles, from the very basic to the very decorative.

Households used to own a vast array of different pieces, but modern canteens are less lavish: a set of knives, forks, dessert spoons and teaspoons is standard. A simple collection such as this should be enough for every day, but it can be useful to add some extras over

time. Steak knives, for example, are not part of a basic canteen, but will be handy if you eat a lot of red meat; soup spoons are very useful, and dessert forks, though rarely included, are perfect for tea parties.

While good-quality modern cutlery/flatware tends to be expensive, old sets can be incredibly cheap. If you need to supplement your existing collection, scour junk shops, eBay, auction houses and street markets and you might unearth some treasures: enamel-handled teaspoons, perhaps, or pretty bone butter knives. Vintage cutlery may not be as practical as its modern counterparts (it will probably need to be washed by hand, and some pieces may tarnish), but it will bring instant charm and character to your table.

If you want to invest in new cutlery/flatware, try it out before you buy. Each piece should feel well-balanced and the handle should sit comfortably in your hand.

informal setting (above) For a relaxed meal, lay a folded napkin on a plate and top with whatever implements you need.
drip-dry (left) Make sure your cutlery/flatware is dry before you store it to prevent tarnishing. Bone-handled pieces or silver plate should not go in the dishwasher.

divide and rule
(left) Drawer dividers
make for easy and
organized storage –
ideal for cutlery/flatware.
handle it (below left)
For a quirky contemporary
look, seek out vintage
designs made from
modern materials. This
plastic set will add interest
and texture to a tabletop.
bamboo beauties
(below) Inexpensive,
tactile and eco-friendly,
bamboo cutlery is easy
to find and perfect for an
informal or outdoor lunch.

table linen

Many of us today do without tablecloths and even napkins, but these offer the perfect finishing touch for a meal. Both practically and aesthetically, using a tablecloth makes sense. It will protect the tabletop from heat or scratches, reduce noise and limit breakages. Most importantly, a tablecloth can give a very average table the air of something smarter — even a wobbly old trestle looks impressive when topped with a lovely cloth.

Linen used to be the must-have material (hence the generic name), but these days tablecloths come in many different guises: printed cotton, heavy damask and vinyl-coated cloth. Choose something that will suit the occasion. Delicate white linen may be just the thing for a vintage tea, but wouldn't be right for a children's party. Here, vinyl-coated cloth is perfect as it's cheap, cheerful and easy to clean. You don't even need a proper cloth — just buy enough metres of fabric to fit your table.

white on white

(opposite) White table linen needn't be a boring option. Look out for embroidered cloths or those with lace, brocade or embroidered trimmings. They'll bring texture to a table without looking fussy. Choose similarly decorative napkins to match for a special lunch or tea.

natural textures (left)

Unbleached linen or fine hessian/burlap can be cut and hemmed to create wonderfully tactile tablecloths and napkins. Utilitarian and earthy, they bring rustic charm to any tabletop.

curtain cloth (above)

Any interesting fabric can make an inspired table covering. Hunt around in flea markets and second-hand stores for antique bedspreads or pretty vintage printed linen curtains, as here.

blanket stitch (above left) Hand-embroidered napkins bring colour and texture to a tabletop. Make your own by edging squares of coarse fabric with simple stitches. pretty paper (above right) Paper napkins are available in countless designs today. utility chic (opposite) For everyday meals, choose no-frills, easy-wash linen that's functional and fun, such as striped cotton, waffle weave or pretty floral prints.

According to the rules of etiquette, tablecloth overhang should measure 15–20cm/6–8in for breakfast or lunch and 20–30cm/8–12in or more for dinner, but how many of us are really going to get out the ruler? Just use your common sense; an average overhang of about a foot or so is fine, whatever the occasion. An undercloth (sometimes called a silence cloth or a table pad) can help to make the top cloth drape properly and will also provide extra protection against hot dishes. To make your own, buy suitable material online or just cut an old blanket down to size.

You don't need to spend a fortune on a new tablecloth. Keep your eyes open at car boot/yard sales or antiques markets for old linen cloths or sheets, or consider using something more unusual. An old curtain could make an inspired cloth; a swathe of Eastern-style fabric provide the perfect backdrop for an Oriental meal. Alternatively, top the table with lengths of wallpaper or pieces of wrapping paper for a one-off occasion. The paper will look graphic and interesting, and – even better – it won't need washing.

If you want your tabletop left on show, opt for a runner rather than a cloth. These come in countless colours and textures, and will bring a chic modern look to your tabletop. Invest in placemats and napkins to match, if you like, or choose some in contrasting colours and textures for a more decorative effect.

behind glass (opposite) To make a change from conventional vases, dream up alternative ways of displaying flowers. Here, a variety of differently sized glass containers have been filled to the brim with flowers to make a striking modern arrangement.

cute caddies (left) Recycled food packaging, such as glass jars or brightly coloured plastic containers, make quirky and eye-catching flower holders. Here, some vintage caddies make inspired vases for a mixture of alliums, choisya and lilac.

pretty simple (below) If you don't have time to dash to the florist, see what's on offer in your backyard. This shaggy astrantia in a tiny glass vase is as pretty as a picture.

flowers and focal points

The simplest and quickest way to bring a table to life is with flowers. Not only do they add colour and interest to a scheme, but they will also give a special touch to any occasion and need not cost a great deal of money. For tabletop flowers, large structured bouquets aren't necessary. Something simple and subtle works best, even for a smart dinner. Single stems (or even just individual flowerheads) placed in glasses along the centre of the table are far more modern than a stiff, formal display.

Raid the garden or windowbox for suitable specimens. A jug of simple peonies, poppies or even cow parsley is perfect for an informal meal. Choose flowers that complement your tableware, or use them as the starting point for the table's decorative scheme. The soft pink of an orchid can be picked up in a napkin tie or a tablemat, for example, while white anemones or hellebores could form the focal point of an all-white winter lunch table.

If you want to place flowers in the middle of the table, make sure the arrangement is not too tall; your guests should be able to see over it easily in order to chat. If you have created a large and dramatic display, it's best to position it at the end of the table or move it to one side at the start of the meal. Avoid strongly scented flowers, as they can put guests off the food.

sorbet shades (opposite) A focal point needn't be confined to the middle of the tabletop. For a splash of colour overhead, hang vivid paper lanterns above the table. Perfect for an Eastern feast.

flower fountain (this page) Fill a decorative metal egg holder with luscious, vivid flowerheads to create an unexpected, dramatic floral feature.

display case (opposite) A vintage glass cake stand can make a lovely focal point for a teatime tabletop. And filled with delicious things to eat, it can be practical, too. Hunt in flea-markets and second-hand stores for old-fashioned designs, or buy a reproduction piece.

single blooms (right) Just one vivid flowerhead displayed in a dainty pressed-glass tumbler is an appealing floral feature; a row of them, lined up down the length of the table, makes a striking central arrangement.

Ideally, stick to unscented blooms or remove strongly perfumed displays from the table before you eat.

How you present flowers is up to you, but generally, the more creative you are, the more impact the arrangement will have. Instead of the usual bunch of flowers in a vase, experiment with single blooms in tumblers or eggcups, use a large bowl or even a cake stand for a pretty central display. You could even scatter petals across the tabletop. Flowers should be an eye-catching focal point, so play around with different effects and see what works best.

If you're entertaining on the spur of the moment and don't have any flowers to hand, there are countless other ways to create an effective display. Use a cluster of candles of different heights, pieces of glittering glassware or a dramatic candelabra. A large platter of seasonal fruit is another good option. An unusual focal point will bring charm and personality to a table, but don't be tempted to overdo it. The trick is to make sure that all the elements of the tabletop work together in harmony rather than one detail grabbing all the attention.

little lights (left)
Tealights can be popped into any container to make a sparkly focal point. Try to find something that matches your tableware; these little ceramic pots would work perfectly with rustic earthenware.

candles and lighting

Getting the lighting right is crucial when it comes to creating a welcoming, hospitable atmosphere to eat by, and achieving the elusive 'not-too-bright-yet-not-too-dim' light level usually demands a spot of experimentation. There's no magic formula, as the level of light you will require varies depending on the season, the time of day and the brightness of your room, so building a flexible lighting system is key.

A good starting point is to get both overhead lights and table or floor lamps fitted with a dimmer switch so that you can easily and swiftly tweak the lighting levels. Then simply add candlelight. This most ancient of light sources not only casts a magical glow but it works perfectly for any occasion, adding instant warmth and atmosphere.

Candles come in hundreds of different colours, shapes and sizes, so it will be easy to find something to suit. While plain white candles work with any tabletop scheme, colourful ones will add an extra decorative dimension. Choose one tone for a strong visual impact, whether it's all pink or all black; or for a kitsch modern table, mix up a variety of bright colours in a candelabra or in separate candlesticks placed down the middle of the table.

Tiny tealights – the cheapest and humblest candles of them all – can be the most effective when used en masse. Popped into pretty glasses and lined up in a row, or set in little glass holders and scattered randomly around the cloth, they will bring instant sparkle to any tabletop.

coloured candles (left and above) Candlelight brings warmth and atmosphere to any occasion and you can't have too much of it. Choose candles that suit your colour scheme, whether it's all green for Christmas lunch or all black for a dramatic monochrome setting. Alternatively, opt for a multicoloured effect – great for a quirky modern table. Candles can be displayed in all manner of ways, so choose something that works with the occasion: an elegant candelabra for a formal dinner, for example, or a simple tealight popped in a glass jar for a barbecue supper.

candle holders (left and right) Hunt around in flea-markets and second-hand stores for lovely old mercury glass candlesticks or simply use whatever you have to hand. Painted Moroccan tea-glasses make pretty containers for tealights, for example.

decorative details

Often it's the finishing touches that you add to a tabletop that make it your own. While smart china, sleek silverware and glittering glassware will make any table look elegant, it's the last-minute flourishes and personal details that put an individual stamp on it.

A good starting point is a look through your cupboards for any hand-me-down bits and pieces: vintage napkins rings, perhaps, or the silver serving spoons that your granny gave you. Flea-markets or museum stores can yield one-off treasures: antique salt and pepper pots, perhaps, or a beautiful glass salad bowl. There's no formula for successful finishing touches; it's just about adding a few things you love to make the tabletop special.

If you don't want to clutter your tabletop with bits and pieces, there are more subtle ways to personalize the table. Write guests' names on pretty cards or chalk them on slate placemats. Using unusual materials for the cloth, the mats and the coasters (be it embroidered felt or vintage wallpaper) will add a quirky, unexpected edge to the tabletop. Be inventive and have fun.

classy glass (top left) As well as being practical, vintage carafes or decanters can add a decorative dimension to a tabletop and can often be found at bargain prices in flea-markets or at auction.
salt and pepper (above left and left) Find interesting ways to serve seasonings. These vintage metal egg poachers are perfect for coarse sea salt and cracked black pepper; more individual pieces, such as these little silver birds, will add a personal touch.

pretty rings (right) The napkin ring is the perfect dress-up accessory on the tabletop and can add all sorts of sparkle and glamour to a table setting. Whether they are in the shape of a crystal flower (as here), in antique polished silver or just a length of vivid ribbon or brocade, napkin rings bring a welcome decorative element and can jazz up even the plainest white china and table linen.

place cards (below) The best way to personalize a place setting is to give it a name. Handwrite guests' names on cards, tags or even slate tiles, and pop them in the middle of each plate.

glorious garlands (right) Don't reserve your decorative efforts solely for the tabletop – think about how to dress up the rest of the room, too. Pretty garlands are a good way to echo the elements of a table scheme and easy to assemble. Here, pink-tinged rose petals have been strung onto thin wire (fishing line would be a good alternative) and hung in a swag at the window for a fabulous finishing touch.

the occasions

You don't need cupboards full of fancy tableware to put together a fabulous table setting. With a creative eye and some ingenious styling ideas, even the most basic ingredients can be dressed up for any occasion, whether it's a family supper or a formal dinner for twelve.

pretty rustic (opposite) A rough linen cloth, simple tableware and a jugful of meadow flowers give this table an appealingly homespun feel – perfect for a weekend breakfast. If your table is modern and doesn't fit the look, opt for a large cloth as camouflage.

help yourself (right) Serve boiled eggs and rustic wholemeal or sourdough bread in a big earthenware bowl so that people can help themselves whenever they sit down to breakfast. Butter served in a little dish completes the picture – if you decant it the night before, it will be soft enough for spreading by morning.

keep it real (below) For this look, stick to natural, earthy colours and textures, and try to eliminate the modern or mass-produced. Choose prettily packaged food, such as yoghurts sold in little glass jars. Though they might cost you a little more, they'll look far more appealing than plastic pots and can be recycled as vases or tealight holders.

weekend breakfast

Saturday or Sunday morning breakfast is an informal affair, so you want a table that's relaxed and inviting. Instead of a glossy contemporary look, opt for a softer, country-kitchen feel, with an emphasis on natural colours and textures. Modern packaging will look out of place, so banish cereal boxes and plastic cartons, and bring out the rustic and the homemade.

Whether you set the breakfast table the night before or in the morning, spend a few minutes on the presentation. Even the simplest table can make an impact if it's well planned.

For a laid-back, laissez-faire feel – just what you want at at the weekend – set a stack of simple crockery at each place, including both plates and bowls, so that people can help themselves to whatever they want. Old-fashioned earthenware is perfect (and can be picked up cheaply in flea-markets or at auction), but more modern pieces – such as bamboo bowls – can be mixed in, too. The key is to keep the colours and textures natural and earthy to give you that rural feel; you could even serve coffee in bowls, French-style, to complete the picture.

Decanting food into pretty containers couldn't be easier to do and will make a big difference to the look of the table. Transfer cereals into glass storage jars (this will also help them to stay fresh), decant milk into a stoneware jug and spoon jams into Kilner jars (it will look homemade). Lastly, a jug of simple cottage-garden flowers will add the right finishing touch.

pretty details (right) Against a plain background of natural colours and simple shapes, a few subtle decorative details will add visual texture. On this table, the floral border of a china bowl and the fine grain of a bamboo dish stand out against the neutral backdrop, while pretty vintage tiles – picked up for a song in a second-hand shop/thrift store and used, ingeniously, as coasters – add another layer of pattern.

mix and match

(left and below) For this informal breakfast table, any collection of china would fit the bill as long as it is simple and understated. Think about combining different textures to add interest. With their natural colour and irregular shapes, these bamboo bowls, for example, make a perfect addition and provide a good counterpoint to the vintage-style china. Eco-friendly and inexpensive, bamboo tableware is becoming increasingly popular and easy to find online or in chainstores.

pretty posy

(above) Nothing will do more to liven up your tabletop than a bunch of flowers. Raid the garden, if you have one, for blooms (or even just greenery) that will go with the rest of your table, and don't spend hours arranging them. A simple jugful of pretty flowers, such as the scabious and cow parsley shown here, is all you need.

lazy brunch

A stack of plates, a mugful of knives and forks, some simple, stress-free food rustled up before guests arrive – what could be easier than a brunch party? The key is to make your table as inviting and adaptable as the occasion itself, with comfortable chairs, a pretty cloth and plenty of serve-yourself elements. Get it right and you might find your breakfast-cum-lunch lingers on till teatime.

a touch of red (right) Picking one or two colours to form the basis of a tabletop scheme helps all the elements hang together. Inspiration can come from anywhere. Here, the red of the flowers in the sprigged floral cloth was the starting point for a red theme, which is echoed in the napkins, strawberries and flowers.

easy tableware (left and below) With its gather-round-the-campfire connotations, vintage enamelware is just right for an informal brunch. Original pieces can be picked up second-hand, but can now reach high prices; repro items are less expensive, but may not have quite the vintage appeal.

help yourself (left) Including help-yourself elements at a brunch party is a good idea, whether it's cutlery stashed in a mug, or platters and bowls piled with delicious things to eat. Allowing guests to serve themselves means less work for you and makes everyone feel easy and relaxed.

pastel shades (above) Enamelware – the first Technicolor kitchenware to be mass-produced – comes in a variety of lovely vintage hues. Look online to find pretty teapots, cups and plates like these ones, which will work with the rest of your tableware.

A leisurely brunch has to be the most relaxed of all social occasions. This informal meal comes with none of the expectations of a proper Sunday lunch and none of the stress of last-minute cooking, so you have plenty of time to enjoy preparing the table. First, choose a cloth or fold a piece of favourite fabric to fit. Brunch is not a formal affair, so don't restrict yourself to white linen; a pretty striped or floral cloth can make the whole room feel cheerful. Use simple, everyday tableware that can either be laid at each place or stacked at one end of the table. Cutlery/flatware can be piled into jars, jugs or mugs, allowing guests to help themselves. For a strong decorative theme, pick out one or two tones from the cloth and repeat them in the accessories. Here, soft pink napkins and vivid flowers echo the reds in the fabric and give a cohesive look to the table. For a quirky twist, introduce some unexpected elements: fill a colander with strawberries, for example; use a mug for flowers or a vintage school slate as a mini tray. The final ingredients? Good friends and good food.

fresh flowers (above and right) Brighten up your tabletop with brilliant blooms. Here, snapdragon stems and a bunch of roses add a splash of vivid colour. Don't feel you have to stick to vases – mugs, Kilner jars, even drinking glasses make interesting containers.

not-just-for-coffee mugs (below) Old enamelware mugs make perfect containers for snacks, forks and even flowers. It doesn't matter if they are not pristine – the odd bit of chipped enamel only adds to their vintage charm.

personal touch

(above and right) With just a little effort, it's easy and inexpensive to create eye-catching and original place settings. Use stencil ink to stamp individual numbers (or images) onto plain paper napkins (if you use a stencil sponge, it shouldn't run) or write guests' names on luggage tags and tie them to the vintage kitchen utensils.

picnic in the park

Just because you're eating on your knees doesn't mean you can't make an occasion of it. With just a little thought and effort, you can turn an impromptu picnic into a memorable event. First, choose the perfect spot — in the shade of a willow tree or under an arbour, for example — then spread out a soft rug on the grass and frame the area with a floaty fabric canopy. A few branches, a length of muslin and a bit of daisy-chain decoration will instantly transform a corner of the park into your own little oasis.

pretty special (opposite and above). Dress your picnic rug as you would your table – with an eye for visual impact. Choose a subtly coloured rug, then echo its colours in the tableware. Here, a palette of soft greens, creams and whites ties the elements together. If you are serving more than finger food, bring along plastic or bamboo cutlery, which is practical and lightweight.

comfort is key (opposite) A rug with a waterproof backing will keep you dry however damp the terrain; if you don't have one, use a ground sheet underneath the top layer for extra protection. Bring some comfy cushions, too, if you have space.

set up camp (below) A length of muslin and a ball of string can easily be squeezed into a hamper and will allow you to transform your picnic spot with an impromptu canopy. Throw the fabric over low branches or make your own ad hoc frame and finish off with some pretty daisy-chain trimmings.

Portability and practicality are key when you're picnicking, but that doesn't mean you have to make do with throwaway cups and ugly plastic plates. Don't bring out your best china — there might be breakages, after all — but gather together pretty utility pieces, such as enamelware dishes and mugs, that look good and that won't weigh you down.

To make life easy, invest in rugs, baskets and hampers with handles and encourage the kids to help with the carrying. If you've room, stuff in a cushion or two — comfort can be an issue when you're sitting on the ground. And remember to bring along folding chairs for older members of the party.

bring a bottle (above) A vintage milk crate makes a perfect carrier for picnic drinks and adds to the pretty, old-fashioned aesthetic. To avoid spillages, serve drinks in individual bottles rather than glasses.

summer barbecue

On a warm summer's day, what could be better than an impromptu barbecue? It won't need much planning and can be far more convivial than a sit-down dinner party. Make sure you have plenty of comfortable seating and enough light to eat by if it's an evening event. Then, throw on a cloth and stack the table with everything your guests might need. For maximum impact, come up with a decorative theme for the tabletop, such as this seaside-inspired style. It's easy to put together and looks fantastic.

keep it on ice (left and below)

Cold drinks are a must on a hot summer's day, but keeping bottles in the fridge calls for endless trips indoors. A better solution is to store bottles and cans beside the table in large buckets filled with ice and water. You don't need to use conventional containers – mini galvanized-metal flowerpots make cute coolers for individual bottles of beer.

plain sailing (opposite) An

outdoorsy, nautical theme is ideal for a barbecue and is also easy to assemble. Throw on a stripy cloth, pile food and cutlery into camping containers and use rope and mini sailing clasps for napkin ties (most ship chandlers should stock a wide selection).

good-looking glasses (right)

Just because you are eating outside doesn't mean you have to restrict yourself to dull glassware. A collection of coloured or etched tumblers or wine glasses will bring a pretty, feminine touch to the table and add visual interest. It's a good idea to put large jugs of water on the table, too, to make refills easy.

A nautical theme is perfect for alfresco eating, and very simple to put together. Buy a ready-made cloth or invest in a length of stripy material. Deckchair fabric is ideal and comes in jolly designs; vinyl-coated cloth will give you a practical wipe-down finish. Top with robust tableware and serving dishes (army surplus or camping supply shops are good places to look), and add some shore-side touches: a pebble at each corner of the cloth; shells as salt and pepper pots; napkins tied with rope and sailing clasps. Citronella candles will deter mosquitoes, while lidded serving dishes keep wasps at bay. And the food? Something simple, delicious and easy to prepare so you can sit down and enjoy the occasion as much as your guests.

seaside style (above left) Use pretty pebbles as weights at the corners of your cloth to stop it blowing up in the wind. They'll cost you nothing and add an authentic beachy touch to the table. shell seasoning (above right) Finally, a way to put those bags of holiday shells to good use: turn them into dishes for sea salt and pepper. carry on camping (below left and opposite) Sturdy camping tins make inspired serving dishes for bread, fruit or even cutlery/flatware and add to the informal, outdoorsy feel. lantern light (below right) At an evening barbecue, it is important to have enough light. Place garden flares around the table (though not too close); hang strings of fairy lights in tree branches and use plenty of candles on the table. Pop them inside storm lanterns or any glass container for safety's sake, and also to shelter them from the wind.

fresh flowers (opposite) Flowers bring a tabletop to life, and often the simpler the arrangement, the better. A jug of seasonal flowers makes any table more inviting and 'dressed up'. If the flowers are scented, remove them before you sit down to eat, and keep displays low so guests can talk across the table.

pretty presents (right) Finish off a giftwrapped parcel with a left-over length of vintage braid or antique lace. Thoughtful finishing touches like this always go down well.

pick your own (below) Help-yourself elements on a table create an easy atmosphere at a relaxed family lunch. Instead of laying out the cutlery/flatware at each place setting, stash it in a decorative jug or bowl, or pile it on napkins at the end of the table so that guests can help themselves to whatever they need.

mother's day lunch

Mother's Day is the perfect occasion for a dreamy, springlike table. Choose a light and simple colour scheme — whites, creams and soft natural shades work well together, and will make the tabletop look fresh and pretty. Keep the background clean and understated. Use a plain white cloth, or leave the table bare; then add decoration in the form of scalloped white plates and feminine glassware.

herbs on show (above left) Table arrangements needn't always be a conventional vase of flowers. Sprigs of zingy green basil seem too pretty to be left in the kitchen, and bring a quirky, informal look to this tabletop. napkin ideas (above right) A new spin on the old-fashioned idea of napkin arranging. Here, cutlery/flatware has been tucked into a folded napkin and a spike of rosemary acts as a scented decorative accent. single blooms (below left) If you have any snapped-off flowerheads, use them as decoration. Just a single bloom wired to the bottom of a glass will make a perfect finishing touch. bow and butterfly (below right) Rather than sticking to standard place cards, think of innovative ways of indicating where guests should sit, such as a pretty ribbon and ornamental wired butterfly tied to the back of the chair.

Whatever food you are serving for Mother's Day lunch, make the table girly. This occasion provides the perfect excuse for indulging in frills and feminity: florals, butterflies and bows would all work here, so dust down your granny's scallop-edged china, bring out some shapely glassware and, above all, think pretty.

To prevent the overall effect becoming too twee, keep the background simple. Use a plain white cloth or leave the table bare or topped with a simple runner. And keep the colour scheme bright and light. Whites, pale pastels and soft neutrals work well together and will not only make the tabletop look fresh and inviting but provide the perfect backdrop for the decorative dinnerware and flowers.

make it special Unexpected elements, such as a posy of flowers tied to the back of a chair, will make any dining table pretty. Opt for robust varieties like lavender or salvia that won't wilt before the end of the meal, and use a simple ribbon that complements the flowers.

make it inviting (opposite)

Think of simple but innovative ways to lay the table that take it beyond the everyday. Here, linen runners have been laid horizontally across the table, forming the basis of a chic modern setting and doubling up as tablemats. The colour scheme of earthy browns and zesty greens gives a sophisticated yet natural look to the tabletop; a theme that is highlighted with horticultural touches: garden twine used as napkin ties; place cards with dainty plant motifs and bowls full of greenery.

take your place (right)

Place cards work well when they tie in with the rest of the tabletop. These plant motif cards, for example, pick up on the surrounding natural theme. To recreate the effect, buy ready-made cards or make your own using stencils, stamps or children's drawings. Punch a hole in one corner and tie the cards to linen napkins using garden twine or string.

easy family lunch

Sitting down to eat together as a family is something we do less often nowadays, but it's a habit worth reviving. A sociable family meal around the table beats a TV dinner hands down, and by making an occasion of a weekend lunch, it can be a pleasure rather than a chore. Dress up your everyday tableware and linen with placemats, decorative place cards, pretty napkins and flowers from the garden. If the table looks inviting, everyone will want to gather round it.

To make table dressing easy for any occasion, it is worth investing in a few tabletop staples. Basic essentials, such as a good cloth or some linen table runners, can be brought out again and again and adapted to create any number of different settings. Choose neutral, natural colours so that you don't limit your colour options, and buy napkins that will work with a variety of tabletop schemes. Here, the soft greens and browns of the table linen form the basis of a smart, garden-themed table, and the natural texture of the raffia-wrapped glasses and the garden twine fits in perfectly. This is the kind of practical and simple setting you can roll out for any family meal, but equally you could easily tweak the look and make it different. Add some glossy black or red plates for an Eastern supper, perhaps, or team the natural colours and textures of the table linen with shiny white plates and chrome accessories for a more contemporary feel. A family meal should be a relaxed and enjoyable occasion, so don't skimp on the details just because you haven't got guests. Put jugs of water on the table so that drinks can be easily topped up, create an eye-catching focal point with sculptural flowers or twinkling candles and add some homemade place cards.

layer on texture (opposite) As well as thinking about the look of your table, consider the tactile elements, too. A rich and inviting combination of different textures can be the making of a tabletop. Here, matt ceramic plates contrast with gleaming metal knives and forks, while linen is teamed with coarse raffia – striking textural combinations that complement the natural colour scheme.

graphic greenery (right) In place of the usual flowers, a bunch of wild grasses and shaggy seedheads makes for an intriguing sculptural arrangement. Scour the garden for ideas or visit a florist to see what's on offer. A zingy all-green arrangement such as this one is perfect for a natural scheme, and means it's the shape and form rather than the colour of the plants that attract attention.

easy refills (left) A large jug of water is an essential at any table, allowing people to top their glasses up easily. This recycled glassware with raffia details adds yet more texture to the table.

all in the detail (left) These woven mats bring interest to the setting and also provide cushioning between the bowl and plate. Handmade from strips of ribbon woven together, they look chic and expensive, but actually cost next to nothing to create.

still life (opposite) Colour isn't the only way to make an impact. This graphic grouping of toning greenery makes a perfect arrangement, even though it's all one shade. The plants themselves are common garden species – green hydrangea heads in the bowls; allium seedheads and twisted grass in the brown jug – but cleverly displayed they make a dramatic focal point.

easy eating (left) Serving food in wide shallow bowls rather than on plates will make any occasion feel informal.

flower power (right) Choose flowers to suit the season and mood. Good alternatives would be coloured hydrangea heads, twisted Chinese bamboo, agapanthus and alliums in flower.

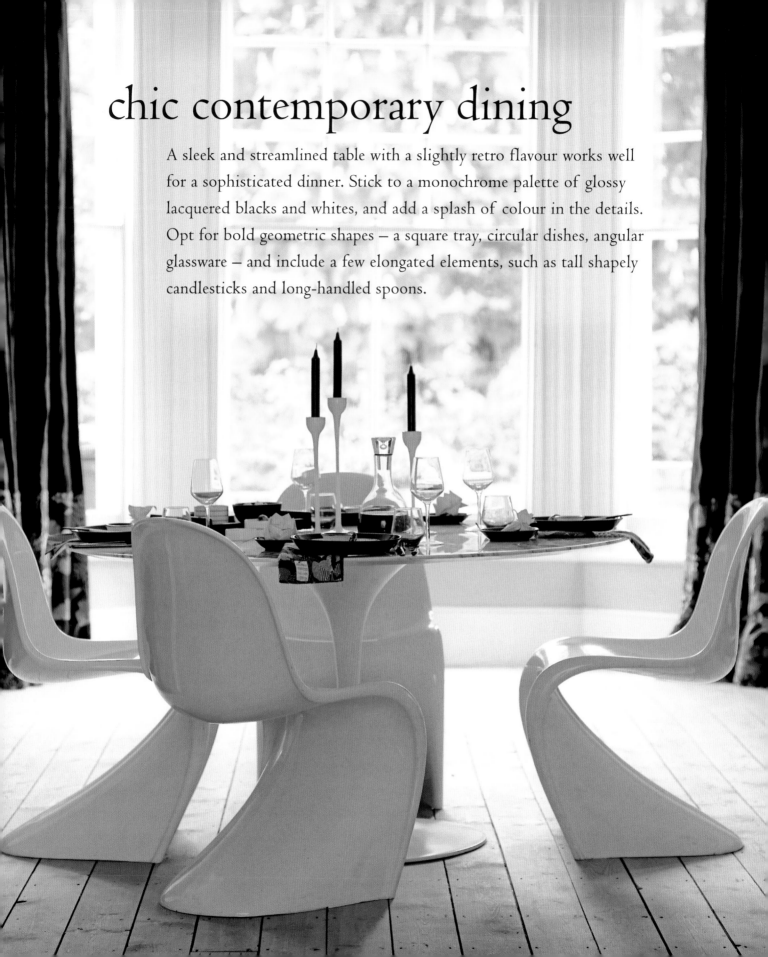

chic contemporary dining

A sleek and streamlined table with a slightly retro flavour works well for a sophisticated dinner. Stick to a monochrome palette of glossy lacquered blacks and whites, and add a splash of colour in the details. Opt for bold geometric shapes – a square tray, circular dishes, angular glassware – and include a few elongated elements, such as tall shapely candlesticks and long-handled spoons.

monochrome mood

(this page) A black and white scheme is perfect for a chic modern setting. If you don't have any black tableware, use dark placemats or napkins to create a bold contrast to white plates, and add the shade elsewhere on the table – black candles, perhaps, or bowls of black olives. Soften the look with minimal decorative touches, such as a pretty paper flower and vibrantly pattered napkins.

Sleek, glossy surfaces are what's needed for a chic modern tabletop, so keep pretty table linen in the drawer and opt for retro elegance. If your table is more country kitchen than bachelor pad, top it with black or white vinyl-coated cloth to create a glossy surface. Team white dinnerware with gleaming dark ceramics (black is ideal) and opt for chunky modern glassware. Angular, retro shapes work best with this look, so choose oblong plates and lacquered trays to serve food and use graphic geometrics at each place setting (a circle on a square on a circle, for example). This is a bold, minimal look, so decoration should be limited. Just a touch, however – a dramatic patterned napkin or a white paper flower – will finish it off perfectly.

glamour and gloss (opposite) This look is all about sleek lines. Plastic Verner Panton chairs and a marble-topped Saarinen table are perfect, but if you don't have the designer furniture, simply add high-gloss accessories: lacquered trays, gleaming candlesticks or glinting modern glassware.

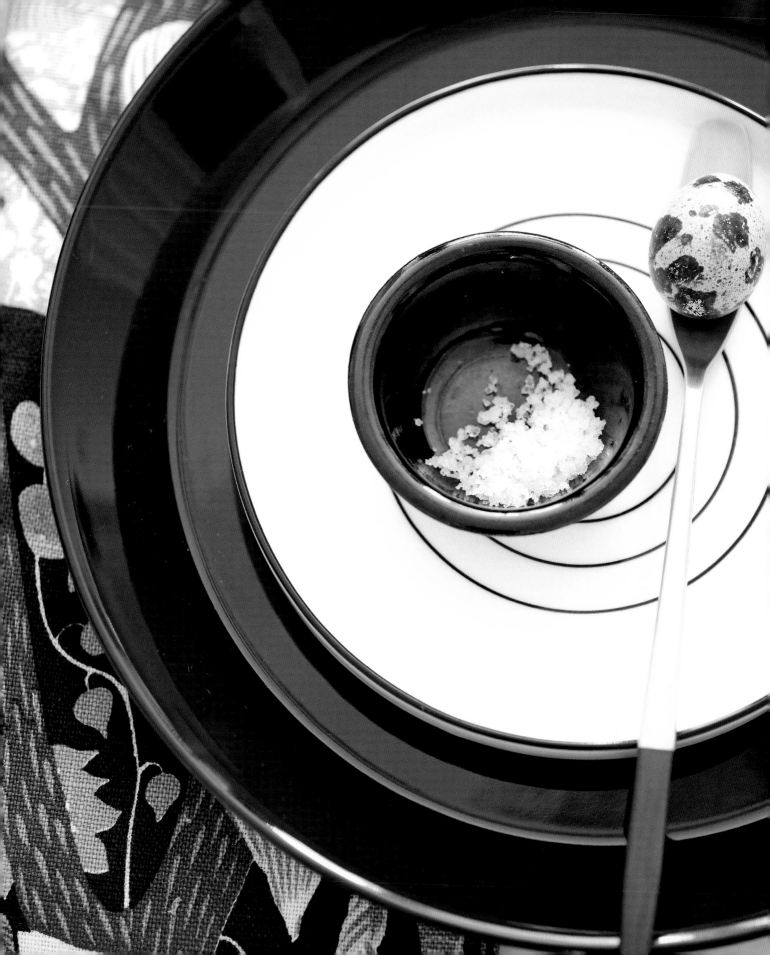

circles and squares (this page and opposite) Create striking contrasts with glossy white and black china, and combine different geometric shapes in graphic arrangements to turn each place setting into a mini masterpiece. A few taller elements, such as these shapely white candlesticks and the chunky modern carafe, will give the setting height, and also work well as a non-floral focal point for the table.

christmas lunch

There's last-minute wrapping to do and a mountain of potatoes to peel, so how do you make time for the table? Easy. Do it in advance and keep it simple. The prettiest Christmas tables aren't piled with expensive china and glitzy trimmings; they are simply dressed and inviting. The ingredients? Warm hues, cosy textures and sparkling candlelight. Now all you have to worry about is the turkey…

cosy christmas table

(opposite) A simple table can still be festive, so take inspiration from the Scandinavians, who have honed the homespun Christmas look to perfection. Stick to natural colours and textures. An antique linen cloth or a blanket will make a tactile tablecloth. Top it with creamy dinnerware and twinkling candles.

decorative details (left and

below) Conjure up a Christmassy atmosphere with a few festive flourishes. These pretty copper cake tins – brilliant containers for candles – bring a quirky edge to the table, while a wooden snowflake adds a subtle seasonal touch.

decorative drinks (this page) Christmas is the perfect time for a glass of warming glühwein. Serve it in little glass tumblers, finished with handmade felt glass cosies to protect the fingers. To make the cosies, cut a length of felt to fit your glass and secure the ends with a couple of stitches or even staples. Finish off with a length of pretty Christmas ribbon. Prost!

make it personal (above) By making your own accessories, you can create an original table setting to use time and again. For this look, choose felt in warm, natural shades and use a thicker version for the placemat to provide extra protection. Add some simple cross-stitch detailing if you have time. Place cutlery/flatware on little chopping boards and finish with a wooden tree decoration for an understated festive touch.

You don't need to buy lots of festive ephemera for the Christmas table. With a little pre-planning, it is easy to rustle up the ingredients for an inviting setting. Track down an antique blanket or a hessian/burlap runner to use as a cloth (the internet is a good hunting ground), then top this with simple, warm-coloured dinnerware, wooden accents and handmade accessories. Get creative and make your own placemats and napkin rings out of felt. It is easy to do – you don't need to be an expert seamstress – and will not only give a personal touch to the table but also cost little.

Wrap tumblers, too, with a felt cosy so that you can serve hot spiced wine at the start of the meal.

Against this warm backdrop, add a splash of colour and pattern: some red candles or a sprig of holly berries; a pretty ribbon; a tree decoration tied onto the stem of a glass or the handle of a fork. And then light the candles. Nothing can create a Christmassy atmosphere better than candlelight, so use as many as you dare: tall red tapers as a dramatic focal point; creamy pillar candles and sparkly tealights to cast a warm glow at each place setting or at the end of the table.

handmade cards (below) These cross-stitched place cards demand a little effort, but are a perfect finishing touch. Using a grid of small squares, mark the name of each guest in pencil on pieces of folded card. Then use embroidery thread and a medium-sized needle to stitch mini crosses in each marked-out square to complete the name.

it's a wrap (above) Custom-made napkin rings tie in with the placemats and glass cosies. Choose felt in a shade that complements the rest of the setting, cut a strip long enough to wrap around your napkin and secure it with a stitch or two. You could use pinking shears to create a more decorative edge.

tealight tins (opposite) Nothing is more Christmassy than candlelight. Here, tealights are placed in fluted copper tart tins. Sweet and sparkly, they instantly make the tabletop look warm and inviting.

kiss kiss (right) Red and cream is a classic Christmas colour combination and these dainty cross-stitches finish the placemat off perfectly. Cross-stitch is easy to do and very effective, but for a different look you could blanket stitch all around the edge of the placemat or, if you're an experienced embroiderer, create a border of leaves or flowers.

in the pink (opposite and right)
Summertime outdoor entertaining gives you the opportunity to make the most of your garden when it's looking its best. Use the colours around you as inspiration for the tabletop scheme. Here, the brilliant pink of a bold feature wall is repeated in the cushions and the table flowers to create a vibrant, energetic theme. For extra atmosphere, tealights tucked into glass pots are suspended above the table with vivid fuchsia ribbon.

garden lunch

There's something special about eating outdoors. It lends an informal Mediterranean air to any occasion and makes everyone — even the host — feel relaxed. Whether you've a roof terrace, a tiny backyard or a rambling country garden, alfresco entertaining can be the perfect solution for a summer lunch party, and dressing the table couldn't be easier. Keep the look pared down but pretty with simple china, decorative glassware and lots of good food. Then just pile on the flowers…

the name game (below left) Head to your local nursery to find plant tags to use as ingenious place cards. Whether wooden, plastic or metal, they'll bring a pretty and unexpected look to each place. potted plants (below centre) You don't need to worry about arranging flowers for an alfresco lunch – use what you already have to hand. Potted herbs and plants in galvanized-metal buckets look completely at home on a garden table, while individual blooms peeping out of miniature flowerpots add a pretty finishing touch. in the details (below right) It's always nice to have the odd one-off element on a tabletop, whether it be a handmade dish or a vintage treasure. Both appealing and practical, these little salt and pepper pots also fit the outdoorsy, garden theme of the rest of the table. petal power (opposite) Each place setting is accessorized with a single pretty pink cosmos head and a floral napkin with a naive, colourful design that contrasts beautifully with the soft blue plates.

An alfresco lunch should be a light-hearted, informal affair, so keep things casual. Leave the table uncovered and serve food on platters or big dishes so that guests can help themselves. Eating in the garden should be a stress-free, convivial occasion, but there are practicalities to consider. First, if it's a sunny day, make sure there's enough shade over the table. If you don't have a parasol, rig up a canopy with a length of muslin or move the table beneath a tree. Secondly, supply cushions. Outdoor seating, whether benches or chairs, isn't generally very comfortable, and extra padding may be welcomed. Invest in some tie-on cushion pads or bring indoor cushions outside. Finally, scare off those insects. Light a citronella candle and protect food with lids or pretty covers.

classic elegant dining

For a special occasion, pull out all the stops and dress your table up to the nines. You don't need fine china and crystal glasses (though if you have them, make the most of them) – the key to a beautiful table is how you dress it, not what you dress it with. Do the groundwork first: polish the table, buff up the dining chairs and throw on a beautiful cloth or runner. Getting the background right makes all the difference. Then choose a colour scheme – a pale, sugared-almond palette is best for easy-on-the-eye elegance.

natural selection (above and opposite) Flowers can provide the inspiration for a table's colour scheme or, as here, create pops of colour against a pale background. For this formal look, you want structured blooms that hold their shape, such as these pink dahlias with their pompom heads. Use tall vases for dramatic effect and move them to one side once the meal is underway.

For sophisticated dining, it's hard to beat white or cream china – it's elegantly understated and goes with everything. To recreate this table, layer the tableware at each place (a stack of plates will instantly give a more formal look to the table), then supply glasses for the drinks you are serving (up to a maximum of three).

If a decorative scheme is plain and pale, it's a good idea to add some visual texture in other ways. Here, a length of embossed wallpaper has been used as a table runner to introduce subtle pattern to the tabletop. Additional details, such as the moiré-effect napkins and the fine flocked paper placed on each plate, further develop the multi-textured look. Colour accents assume more importance in a neutral scheme – they're needed to prevent it becoming bland. Don't pick vivid shades that create too much contrast. Instead, choose two subtle complementary shades (soft pink and green, for example) and repeat these two tones in the tabletop details: the flowers, napkin rings and place cards.

dressing up (below) When it comes to fine dining, white china is elegant, understated and versatile. It also offers a blank canvas that's great fun to dress up. Here, at each setting a piece of patterned paper has been topped with a handwritten place card. The ribbon bow echoes the hue of the candy-pink pompom dahlias in the middle of the table.

complementary colour (above) Hydrangea sprigs have been wired onto silver napkin rings and echo the pink and green colour combination of the tabletop flowers. Any robust blooms – roses or orchids, perhaps – would work, as their sturdy stems are easy to attach.

adding interest (opposite) This table is the perfect example of how texture and colour can bring a table to life. Vibrant touches of pink and green lift the calm, neutral tones of the room, while textured papers and fabrics add subtle pattern to the scheme.

statement flowers (left) When you get the chance, go for the grand gesture. Choose stately stems, such as these lime-green molucella, or structured blooms like the pink dahlias. If you choose two varieties, make sure they complement each other in colour and shape. Opt for glass vases, which won't detract from the impact of the flowers.

textural tabletop (this page) Looking
just like a vintage embroidered cloth, this
embossed wallpaper makes an ingenious runner.
Even better, it doesn't need washing afterwards.
Make sure you also use mats to protect the table
from hot plates.

soft focus (opposite) Tweak a conventional
table setting to make it your own. Here, placemats
have been laid vertically rather than horizontally
to give a softer look to the table.

vintage tea

Nothing can beat the charm of an old-fashioned tea table laden with delicious things to eat, and it couldn't be simpler to achieve. The ingredients? A simple white linen cloth piled high with frills, florals and fairy cakes. It doesn't matter if nothing matches – that's all part of the quirky vintage appeal.

pretty old-fashioned

(this page) A vintage tea party is the perfect occasion for making the most of pretty traditional tableware. Sprigged porcelain teacups, lacy napkins, bone-handled knives and dainty cake forks all fit the bill perfectly. Keep the colours pale and pretty – faded pinks, delicate lilacs and soft blues, set against white or cream – and favour gently curved shapes over straight lines or hard edges.

Creating a dainty, old-fashioned tea table couldn't be easier, for you are likely to have much of what you need to hand. Start with a white or cream tablecloth (or an old linen sheet will do), then rummage through your cupboards for hand-me-down teacups or china plates with pretty fluted edges and floral motifs. Alternatively, look in junk shops or auction rooms for suitable pieces – a Victorian teapot, perhaps, or a boxed set of mother-of-pearl-handled pastry forks. Don't go for matching sets: odd teacups and plates will be less expensive, and for this look an eccentric mix is what you are after. Department stores, too, are good places to look – it's easy to pick up the perfect finishing touch, whether it's a pretty pressed-glass cake stand or crocheted doilies.

tea party tabletop (opposite) With a nostalgic nod to your grandmother's tea table, introduce frills, flowers and chintzy china for your vintage tea. Don't forget to offer perfumed Earl Grey tea and delicious traditional cakes.

let them eat cake (opposite) A pressed-glass cake stand is an eye-catching focal point, especially when piled high with cupcakes iced in pastel shades. Buy ready-made cakes or make your own, topped with swirls of buttercream and sugarpaste flowers. If your cake stand is too low, improvise and add another layer by popping a glass saucer on top of a teacup.

mismatched mix (below) The great thing about this tabletop is that you don't need a matching tea set to start with. Mix your vintage pieces with junk shop/thrift store finds to create an appealingly eccentric mix.

Pretty elements are what you want on a vintage tea table, so think about the details. Choose napkins with decorative trims or customize plain ones with lace ribbon and floral sprigs. It's easy to do and, for this look, you don't need to worry about going over the top. Use vintage silver teapots, china jugs and teacups to hold old-fashioned flowers in pastel colours – peonies or hydrangeas are perfect. Then have fun with the decorative details: tealights in fluted cupcake cases or wedding sugar lumps served on silver spoons. And to eat? Dainty cupcakes or a homemade sponge oozing with jam and cream.

pastel hues (above) Sugar pinks, pale lilacs, knocked-back blues; pretty faded shades against cream or white are ideal for a vintage tea table. Choose your flowers first and then add details to match. Here, the pink tealights pick out the colour of the blowsy peony blooms.

beautiful blooms (left) Pretty flowers are a must on a vintage tea table and look good displayed in everything from china jugs to silver teapots. Frothy old-fashioned blooms in sugary shades, such as the peonies and popcorn hydrangeas shown here, will work best.

spoonful of sugar (above) Finish off your vintage-style tabletop with pretty details, such as this row of wedding- favour sugar lumps, displayed on silver spoons. They don't just look sweet, they taste it too!

primary colours (opposite)
A party table needn't be a testament to
bad taste. Conjure up a creative, cheerful
look that both you and the kids will love,
with bright party plates, delicious finger
food and fun decorations. String up a
ribbon curtain or a length of bunting
to add to the atmosphere.

goody buckets (right) Offer an
innovative alternative to cheap plastic
goody bags: these colourful mini buckets,
filled with little gifts, will go down a storm
and can be reused afterwards. Add a
special name tag tied on with string
so that they don't get muddled up.

bright ideas (below) Even a kid's
party can have a colour scheme, but
don't be subtle. Mix colourful melamine
or paper plates with contrasting paper
napkins and place mats. Choose napkins
and serving bowls in zingy, shout-out
shades then add streamers, fun
accessories and balloons.

children's party

Ice-cream, pass-the-parcel, a bunch of balloons at the
front gate — nothing beats a kids' party for good, old-
fashioned fun. Though it may be tempting to buy in
ready-made party packs with cartoon-character paper
plates and plastic cups, decorating the table yourself
is more rewarding and less expensive. Play around with
brilliant colours and creative ideas for a child-friendly
look that will impress the adults, too.

necklace names (opposite)

Treat the tabletop with as much care as you would for an adult party and make each place setting look pretty. Indicate where guests should sit with a necklace of threaded letter beads: not only a novel spin on place cards that kids will love, but also a perfect party keepsake.

sugar and spice (left and right)

Party food should be easy to eat and very appealing. Serve savoury goodies first (mini sandwiches, crunchy carrot batons and cheese straws), then bring out the sweet stuff. Fill little bowls with jelly beans or miniature cookies and place them at each end of the table. For drinks, avoid flimsy paper cups, which always get knocked over. Older kids will do better with sturdy mini bottles (though if they're glass, watch out for breakages). Finish each off with a name tag and a drinking straw to make them extra special.

think practical (below)

Lightweight , inexpensive plastic knives, forks and spoons are perfect for a children's party. Stack them in colourful cups on the tabletop so that guests can help themselves as necessary.

Let's be honest: there's going to be mess at a children's party, so prepare yourself in advance. Place the table on a floor that's easy to clean (or, even better, move it outside) and cover it with a practical cloth. Vinyl-coated cloth is perfect; it comes in a multitude of different designs and can be bought by the metre. Get your children involved in choosing tableware, paper napkins and plastic cutlery in rainbow shades. Pretty paper plates are widely available and will save on the washing-up later. Finally, add a few just-for-fun details, such as miniature windmills or a sprinkling of cut-out confetti. Cover the table with dishes of easy and appealing things to eat: tiny sandwiches, sausages on sticks and mini marshmallows.

pretty smart (opposite) It's often easier to host a baby shower in the sitting room rather than around the dining table. The seating tends to be more comfortable and chairs can be pulled together to create a more intimate and informal grouping. Use a coffee table or even a low chest to hold food and drinks, and scatter lots of cushions. The scheme here is subtle and pretty, with baby pink and blue details set against a smart neutral background.

pink and blue (right) Pretty pastel napkins make the perfect finishing touch at a baby shower. Wrap each one with a strip of delicate paper and a pink or blue ribbon, secured with a safety pin.

tactile tools (below) Sustainable and inexpensive, bamboo cutlery will add a contemporary touch to any table. It can be found in most good homeware stores and on the internet, but you may not be able to use it more than once.

baby shower

More an informal get-together with girlfriends than a party, a baby shower is easy to prepare for. Choose the time slot (morning coffee or afternoon tea work best), plan a stress-free menu and think of cute ways to dress the table. Pastel pinks and blues are the obvious colour choice, but don't overdo it or you'll tip the balance from sweet to saccharine. Keep the overall look pale and pretty, and stick to stylish – albeit baby-themed – accessories.

Even the most basic table can be dressed up with pretty details to make the perfect backdrop for a baby shower. Instead of a cloth, use sheets of fine paper to cover the tabletop. Choose a finish that appeals, whether it be simple sugar paper, crêpe paper or something with more pattern or texture (art supply shops will stock a good selection). Top with homemade paper placemats, which can be customized with pink or blue ribbon to fit the theme, and simple tableware. Paper plates and cups will make life easy if you can find them in the appropriate shades, but white china would also work well. Finish the table with flowers (sweet peas were used here) in simple glass bottles and some lovely things to eat.

littlest things (opposite and above) Little touches make a huge difference to the look of a tabletop and needn't take up much time or effort. Here, a craft knife was used to cut slits along the top of each paper placemat, then a length of blue or pink ribbon was threaded through the slits to create a pretty border.

fragile blossoms (below) Recycled glass jars make good-looking vases. Soak the labels off old jars or bottles and customize with a band of pretty ribbon or paper. Then simply fill with flowers.

pretty pastels
(above and left) Whatever the hour of the baby shower, serve beautifully presented food that fits the theme. Here, iced petit fours were popped into dainty, pastel-hued cupcake cases, while buttery cookies were finished off with pink and blue tissue paper wraps, secured with a mini clothes peg.

gentleman's club (opposite)
Smart and streamlined, this tabletop has a clubby, sophisticated feel. Keep the scheme understated and masculine with dark tones and polished textures. A glossy bare wood table is perfect, but if you don't have one, throw over a deep brown or green cloth or a runner. Keep decorative trimmings to a minimum; a chic, pared-down look is your aim.

wrapped up (right) Even a bottle of beer can be dressed up. Here, palm leaves – found at most florists – have been used as wraps and held in place with little cocktail skewers.

mapped out (below) Make personalized placemats from unexpected materials. Old maps, vintage blueprints or even old sheet music will make any setting interesting. Cut pieces to the appropriate size and get them laminated, if you like, for a glossy, wipe-down finish.

father's day meal

Father's Day is the perfect excuse for a family meal, and with just a little effort you can transform your everyday table into the perfect backdrop for the occasion. You don't need to buy anything special; just opt for a smart, pared-down look and add some personal touches: homemade placemats, perhaps, or hand-drawn place cards. Simple and stylish, it's a scheme you could easily adapt for a lunch or dinner with friends.

Creating a smart Father's Day table doesn't require special dinnerware or accessories. Use whatever you have to hand, but add imaginative touches to take the tabletop beyond the everyday. Keep the background pared down, then think of novel ways to bring personality to the table. One-off placemats, made from old maps, newspapers, vintage comics or sheet music, are easy to make and add a quirky, graphic element to the scheme, as well as providing an instant talking point. Develop the theme further by spelling out your dad's name at the top of the setting with interesting lettering – pieces of vintage type, perhaps, or scrabble tiles. Add napkins and dinnerware in smart complementary colours.

base notes (above and right) Keep the tabletop tones dark and moody for an unfussy, masculine effect. Strong greens and earthy brown tones will create a simple backdrop; splashes of vivid colour and quirky graphic details bring the look to life.

autumnal dinner

Creating a setting that takes the changing seasons as its inspiration gives you the chance to play around with colour, texture and natural produce. With its falling leaves, fruit-filled orchards and palette of golden hues, Autumn provides a glut of decorative ideas. So look around you and come up with a scheme that's as rich and atmospheric as the landscape outside.

Whether you are eating in the kitchen or the dining room, an autumnal dinner should be an informal, bountiful affair – it is harvest time, after all. So dress your table with appealing natural textures and warm colours: chestnut, ochre, russet and gold. If you have a wooden table, use a runner rather than a cloth so that the grain and patina of the wood can be seen. If not, throw on a tablecloth made from tactile woven muslin or linen. For an autumnal touch, you could use two layers of fine fabric and sandwich dried fallen leaves between them, allowing their silhouettes to show through. For a different effect, you could use a length of waxed paper as a runner, but you'll then need extra mats to protect the table from hot dishes.

Top with tableware in warm tones (terracotta or earthenware dishes would be perfect) or customize what you have with simple squares of brown paper as placemats and use dried leaves or sculptural twigs as additional details. Pop tealights into tiny bowls to make the table glow and serve steaming bowls of pumpkin soup and slices of spiced apple pie.

natural touch (left) Earth-toned dinnerware, a wooden table, golden leaves and hints of green – the ingredients for a chic seasonal tabletop couldn't be easier to put together, but the result is very effective.

harvest hues (this page)
To create an inviting, autumnal table,
stick to a palette of warm tones – ochre,
chestnut, conker-brown – then pile on
some natural texture. A wholesome,
homespun feel is the effect to aim for.

pretty pear (opposite) Decorating your autumn table with leaves is easy and effective. Flatten fallen leaves between pieces of greaseproof paper within the pages of a large book and, when dry, use them as doilies or simply scatter on the tabletop. Alternatively, buy pretty leaf skeletons – such as this one – in craft shops and tie with string onto the stalk of an apple or pear.

decorative details (right) The secret to a beautiful table lies in the finishing touches. Using the same cutlery/flatware, tableware and glass, you can create entirely different looks just by tweaking the details. Here, pretty leaves, fresh fruit and the occasional twig lend the tabletop its autumnal air.

tempting textures (left) Wrapped in baking parchment and given a pretty felt leaf tag, these loaves of bread become instantly more decorative.

clever cloth (right) To create an autumnal tablecloth, sandwich leaves between layers of muslin so that they show through. Alternatively, top your table with a sheet of Perspex/Plexiglass to make the effect more dramatic.

supper for two

Even the simplest table can be dressed up for a romantic dinner. Create drama with dark, jewelled colours and low-level lighting, use tactile dinnerware and sparkling, ornate glass, then add a dash of glamorous gold. Against this seductive background, serve luxurious, sensual food: soft fresh figs, succulent strawberries or dark chocolate mousse. And the flowers? Red roses, of course.

To create a romantic atmosphere, the first thing to do is turn the lights down low. Use a dimmer switch or turn off the overheads altogether and just use candles. Camouflage your table with a richly textured cloth – embroidered velvet, for example, or exotic lace. Look in second-hand stores for a length of vintage fabric if you don't have something suitable; it doesn't need to be expensive. Top with toning dinnerware and invest in some pretty vintage glasses (you'll only need two). Sipping wine or champagne from a delicate glass makes all the difference. Add metallic notes for glamour: gilt candlesticks, perhaps; a piece of brocade wrapped round a napkin; or a pair of gold-coloured knives and forks.

glamour glass (above) Pretty vintage drinking glasses create a luxurious effect. Look in second-hand stores for interesting designs; they don't have to match. low lights (above right) Turn off the overhead lights and fill the room with candles. They cast a lovely glow and create instant atmosphere. midas touch (opposite) Any table can be transformed with silver or gold accessories, such as these mercury glass candleholders.

red roses (opposite) It might be the stuff of cliché but it is hard to beat roses for the ultimate romantic finishing touch. You don't need armfuls of flowers to make an impact – displaying a single rose head in a small bowl, as here, can be just as effective. table for two (this page) As there are only two place settings, there is plenty of room on the table for glitz and glamour. To start, throw a richly patterned cloth over the table and then cover it with accessories in jewelled colours and sensuous textures: chocolate-coloured napkins tied with ornate brocade ribbon; pretty, delicate wine glasses; sparkling candles in gleaming holders. Use dark-hued, exotic dinnerware if possible to enhance the moody atmosphere; or camouflage white plates with gold or silver doilies. Now turn off the overhead lights, light the candles and let dusk fall…

cocktail party

If you can't squeeze all your friends around your dining room table, or you have something special to celebrate, throwing a drinks' party is the perfect solution. Send out the invitations well in advance, hire some pretty glassware and decide on a few easy-to-prepare cocktails that look as good as they taste. Dress up your home with flowers and decorative details – just because it's not a sit-down meal doesn't mean you can't go to town on the table setting. And don't forget the food. Beautifully presented canapés will provide the perfect finishing touch.

decorative details (this page)

A splash of colour and pattern will add to the party atmosphere, but don't overdo it. Place a vivid bloom at the base of each glass or scatter petals across the tabletop. Create pretty coasters from textured or patterned papers; it's easy to do and very effective. For a more dramatic touch, hang homemade paper fans from the ceiling. To create a circle, staple two individual fans together.

Though easier to plan than a sit-down dinner, a cocktail party needs some preparation. Decide where you're going to hold it and then move furniture around, if necessary, to free up enough space. Most guests are happy to stand, but make sure there is a quiet and comfortable sitting area where people can retreat if they want to, and provide lots of surfaces for holding drinks. Decorate tables with pretty cloths or homemade coasters and get the cocktails ready in advance so that you are free to greet your guests. Background music can create instant atmosphere, but make sure it's not too loud. Think about the temperature, too; a crowded room can get hot, so lower the heating if you need to or open up the windows.

happy hour (opposite)

A creatively arranged table will be the focal point of a drinks party. Keep the look chic and simple with a colour scheme of vivid pinks and muted greens. Then add some attention-grabbing flowers.

button tags (below) Using vintage buttons is a pretty and practical way to personalize guests' drinks at a party. Look out for appealing and unusual designs in second-hand stores or at auctions and then simply thread individual buttons onto a length of ribbon and tie to the stems of wine glasses or champagne coupes.

serving spoons (above) Oriental china soup spoons are perfect for presenting lime wedges or serving canapés. They cost little, come in countless designs and make a distinctive and modern tabletop feature.

creative coasters (opposite) To make your own coasters, use whatever you have to hand. Here, a band of plain ribbed parchment has been topped with squares of pretty patterned paper to create a striking combination. Dusky pink orchid heads, set at the base of each glass, provide the perfect finishing touch.

serve yourself (right) It's tricky to eat when you are standing up and holding a drink, so any food at a cocktail party should be easy to eat with one hand. Offer round bite-sized canapés and load up tables with lots of help-yourself elements. A dish of olives, supplied with mini bamboo cocktail sticks, always goes down well.

flower filled (right) For an eye-catching party table, dream up innovative ways of displaying flowers. Here, instead of the usual jugs or vases, shapely glass bottles showcase tropical blooms. Half-fill with water, add one or two flowers to each (with stems cut much shorter than usual) and group together on the table to make a striking arrangement.

chin chin (opposite) Whether you are offering your guests champagne, wine or cocktails, make sure you provide soft drinks for non-drinkers and drivers. Create something special just for them so that they don't feel left out: a fruit punch, for example, or a fruity, jewel-toned cordial served in individual bottles.

It's the drinks that take centre stage at this kind of party, so offer a selection. Alongside wine, beer or cocktails, provide a soft-drink option. It needn't be dull. Create a colourful fruit punch or offer bottles of elderflower cordial or old-fashioned lemonade, topped with a drinking straw. Make sure, too, that you provide enough things to eat to mop up the alcohol, particularly if your party is at lunchtime. Canapés don't need to be complicated. (bite-sized crostini, sausages on sticks or mini smoked salmon bagels are all hard to beat) but they should look good and taste delicious. Prepare the food well before the party starts so that there won't be any last-minute panics in the kitchen.

pretty portable (left) By laying each place setting on a little tray, you give everyone the option of relocating en masse to the sofa or the terrace. Top with simple tableware and conjure up a complementary colour scheme. Here, pretty pastel plates and bowls look perfect set against green and white.

simple setting (opposite) Even an everyday supper can be turned into an occasion if you spend a little time making the setting look good. Serve up bread or nibbles in whatever you have to hand – a tactile bamboo steamer, perhaps, or a shiny Indian tiffin tin – and bring in some flowers. Here, voluptuous parrot tulip heads have been popped into jam jars and suspended from a ceiling beam to bring the dining area to life. If you haven't a suitable ceiling support, arrange the flower jars on the table to make an inspired focal point.

relaxed supper

A successful weekday supper for family or friends should be sociable and stress-free, but squeezed in between the homework and feeding the cat, paying bills and washing up the breakfast things, it can fall by the wayside. This easy, go-anywhere setting can be moved wherever you like, even outside. Easy to put together and very appealing, it will allow you to leave the mess behind and make an occasion of the simplest meal. Serve easy comfort foods, pour some wine and everyone will want to join in.

hanging flowers (opposite) DIY decorations can make a big impact. Made using flowerheads, recycled glass jars and a length of string, these hanging jars couldn't be prettier. For a different effect, use other flowers or fill the jars with beautiful shells, decorative beads or twisting grasses.
colour match (below left) Taking a minute to consider the colour combinations of a table setting can make all the difference. Complementary shades, such as these subtle pinks and greens, work well. Boldly contrasting colours – black against white, for example – are just as effective, but in a different way. Try a few alternatives and see which you like best. food on the move (below right) For a go-anywhere table setting, you need portable pieces. A lightweight bamboo steamer and a shiny tiffin tin make perfect serving dishes.

A relaxed supper should be easy to prepare and to clear up, so pick a simple menu and use the minimum amount of tableware. This isn't the occasion for lots of side dishes and dirty saucepans. Choose delicious, one-bowl food that everyone likes. Pasta, couscous or a hearty soup fit the bill perfectly, and can be eaten with just a fork or spoon, so there will be less washing-up later. Small bottles of water are more portable than glasses when you're putting together a go-anywhere table setting like this. Fill empties with tap water and stash in the fridge when you get home from work so that they're cold by suppertime. Finally, add a few pretty elements – just because it's an everyday occasion doesn't mean it can't be special, too.

eastern banquet

With simple tableware in organic shapes, natural textures and rich colours, the Oriental table is perfect for a modern dinner party. Make use of what you have – plain white dinner plates, stoneware bowls or rush tablemats – and then introduce some additional Eastern elements. Throw a length of Oriental fabric across the table, banish knives and forks in favour of chopsticks and fill little rice bowls with all the necessary accoutrements for an Eastern feast – soy sauce, fortune cookies and sachets of hot wasabi.

bring in the bowls (left and below) Although you can use your existing tableware for an Oriental feast, supplement it with a few Eastern pieces to complete the look. Little rice bowls, teacups, sauce and pickle dishes – all these items are easy to get hold of and won't break the bank. Look in Oriental supermarkets for the best bargains or shop online. Alternatively, tweak the traditional Eastern look with a few more quirky elements, such as these little bamboo trays.

keep it low (opposite) Fun and informal, low-level dining makes a change from conventional entertaining, and a coffee table or low bench makes the perfect tabletop. Cover with a length of Oriental-style fabric, surround with a scattering of comfortable cushions and you'll achieve the look in an instant.

finishing touch (right) Decorate the tabletop with simple graphic stems such as these nectaroscordum. And choose a vase that fits in with the rest of the tableware. Dark colours and natural textures are what's called for here.

Blending opulence with informality, an Oriental-style table makes for a relaxed dinner with a difference, and it's easy to put together. Get the basics right first: you'll need a low table and comfortable floor cushions, so consider moving from the dining to the living room to give yourself more space.

If you don't have a low coffee table, improvise and make a dining table from whatever you have to hand – a couple of low laundry chests or a futon base. Whatever you use will be covered, after all. Stick to a neutral colour scheme – shades of bamboo, stone and wood mixed with glossy lacquered black. Add a dash of brilliance in the details: a vivid red cushion cover, perhaps, or a deep pink flower.

oriental ornament (previous pages) Choosing an Eastern theme can give you the chance to indulge in deep colours and exotic textures. Here, an ornately-patterned cloth is topped with deep browns, reds and glossy lacquered blacks to create a rich, inviting tablescape. Deep pink dahlia heads popped into simple bamboo bowls make the perfect finishing touch.

chop chop (left) Chopsticks are a must at any Eastern feast. Invest in some pretty chopstick rests, too, to complete the setting.

tea time (opposite) An Oriental tea party demands serious ceremony, so why not make an occasion of it? Hunt down some traditional Eastern-style teapots (they don't need to be expensive) and then serve a selection of green teas in dainty tea bowls. Japanese and Chinese teas are readily available these days, and many can even be ordered over the internet. Invest in a thermometer, too. The water should be at just the right temperature when you are brewing the perfect cup of Eastern tea.

A dark, exotic colour scheme works well for an Eastern theme, but you could lighten it for a more contemporary look. Replace lacquered black trays and charcoal-coloured teapots with bamboo plates and pale rush placemats; instead of a cloth, use pale linen or pleated paper. You don't need to follow any rules. Mix up Eastern and Western tableware to create your own version of the look, or give a kitsch modern twist to the traditional setting by choosing brilliantly coloured soup spoons or napkins in a quirky Japanese print. The only goal is to create the perfect backdrop for your Eastern feast, whether it be sushi, noodle soup or just a Chinese takeaway.

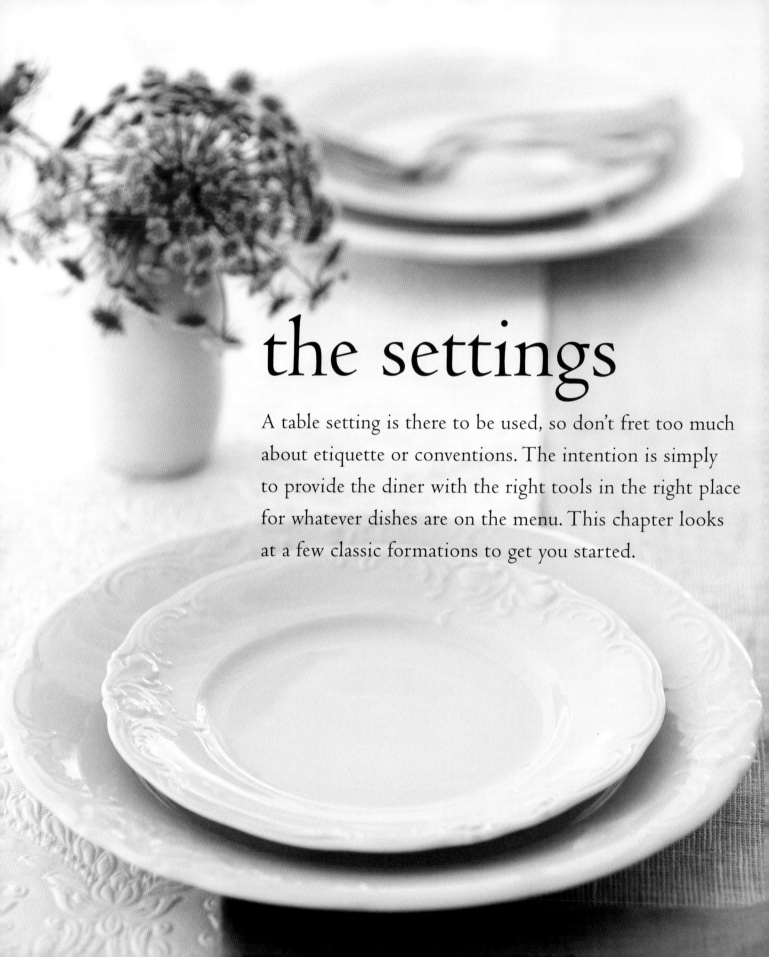

the settings

A table setting is there to be used, so don't fret too much about etiquette or conventions. The intention is simply to provide the diner with the right tools in the right place for whatever dishes are on the menu. This chapter looks at a few classic formations to get you started.

international informal

This basic table setting will work for any informal Western meal and can be adapted depending on the food being served. Cutlery/flatware is positioned in the most convenient place for the diner: dinner fork to the left of the dinner plate; knives and soup spoons to the right and dessert forks and spoons above the plate, with handles facing the hand that will be using them. The glasses are positioned at the top right, with the largest glass (generally the red wine glass) set at the back for neatness.

1 Napkin in a simple fold
2 Dinner fork
3 Dinner plate
4 Dinner knife
5 Soup spoon
6 Dessert spoon
7 Dessert fork
8 White wine glass
9 Red wine glass
10 Water glass

British formal

For a dinner party, you may want to use a more formal table setting involving a wider selection of tableware. In this case, all the cutlery/flatware for the meal can be placed either side of the dinner plate and should be laid from the outside in so that the first-course cutlery/flatware is outermost (and thus most accessible) and the dessert spoon and fork innermost. A side plate for bread can be set to the left, and if you want to supply a butter knife, this can be laid across the plate in line with the edge of the table.

1 Napkin in a simple fold
2 Butter plate
3 Dinner fork
4 Dessert fork
5 Dinner plate
6 Dessert spoon
7 Dinner knife
8 Soup spoon
9 White wine glass
10 Red wine glass
11 Water glass

English afternoon tea

If you are serving a formal sit-down tea, make sure you provide appropriate utensils for whatever food you are offering. You may need a butter knife, a pastry fork and even a spoon for a particularly creamy cake. These implements should all be set to the right of the plate, with the napkin placed on the left (or on top of the plate if you prefer). For a proper afternoon tea, it's imperative to use your very best teacups and saucers; mugs just won't give you the same sense of occasion.

1 Napkin in a simple fold
2 Butter plate
3 Bread knife
4 Dessert spoon
5 Pastry fork
6 Saucer
7 Teacup
8 Teaspoon

American formal

Very similar to the British formal style, the American setting also places cutlery/flatware for each course either side of the dinner plate, working from the outside in. Here, the first course is a fish dish, so the outermost items are a fish knife and fork. Cutlery for the main course and pudding then follow. Americans tend to place bread or salad plates to the top left of the setting rather than at the side. Glasses are set in the standard triangular formation.

1 Napkin in a simple fold
2 Fish fork
3 Dinner fork
4 Pudding fork
5 Dinner plate
6 Dessert spoon
7 Dinner knife
8 Fish knife
9 White wine glass
10 Red wine glass
11 Water glass
12 Butter plate

French formal

Unlike the British and Americans, the French place their cutlery/flatware face down on the table and use a tablespoon for soup instead of a rounded soup spoon. Side plates and butter knives are not required, as bread is placed directly on the table and butter is not generally served. Cutlery/flatware is laid out in a standard Western style, but a knife rest is sometimes used so that the dinner knife can be laid back on the table and reused for the cheese course, which in France is served before the dessert.

1 Napkin in a simple fold
2 Dinner fork
3 Pudding fork
4 Dinner plate
5 Dessert spoon

6 Dinner knife
7 Soup spoon
8 White wine glass
9 Red wine glass
10 Water glass

Chinese informal

A standard Western dinner plate, side plate and bowl can just as easily form part of a Chinese table setting, but a few extra accessories will be required to finish it off. You'll need a handleless teacup for jasmine or green tea; a Chinese soup spoon (ideally one that matches the bowl); a little dish for dipping sauces; chopsticks and a chopstick stand. You may also need an extra rice bowl if you are serving both soup and rice, but this can be brought to the table as needed. And conventional cutlery/flatware should be available for guests who are inexperienced with chopsticks.

1 Dinner plate
2 Chopsticks
3 Chopstick stand
4 Sauce dish
5 Teacup
6 Soup bowl
7 Soup spoon
8 Saucer

Japanese informal

Much like the Chinese setting, the Japanese table requires a number of bowls, dishes and plates for serving all the elements of a Japanese meal. Rice, noodles and soups are served in a bowl; sushi and sashimi, fried and grilled dishes are served on an open plate. Small dishes are needed for sauces and pickles, and a handleless teacup for miso soup. A small jug can also be used for soy sauce so that guests can help themselves. Chopsticks should be positioned right at the front of the setting with the ends pointing towards the left.

1 Rice bowl
2 Chopsticks
3 Chopstick stand
4 Soup bowl

5 Pickle dish
6 Teacup
7 Dinner plate

sources

UK SOURCES

LAURA ASHLEY
www.lauraashley.com
Patterned linens and wallpaper.

C. BEST (FLORISTS)
Flower Market
New Covent Garden Market
London SW8 5NA
020 7720 2306
Metal buckets, candlesticks and vases.

BODIE AND FOU
www.bodieandfou.com
*Modern table accessories, glassware
and candleholders.*

BRISSI
196 Westbourne Grove
London W11 2RH
020 7727 2159
www.brissi.co.uk
Elegant homeware.

CABBAGES AND ROSES
3 Langton Street
London SW10 0JL
020 7352 733
Cabbagesandroses.com
Table linen in vintage-style prints.

CERAMICA BLUE
10 Blenheim Crescent
London W11 1NN
020 7727 0288
www.ceramicablue.co.uk
*Unusual stoneware, recycled glass
platters and slate cheeseboards.*

CLOTH HOUSE
47 Berwick Street
London W1F 8SJ
020 7437 5155
www.clothhouse.com
*Vintage French linens and fabrics such
as felt, canvas, printed cotton, ticking,
ginghams, hessian and jute.*

THE CLOTH SHOP
290 Portobello Road
London W10 5TE
020 8968 6001
www.theclothshop.net
Antique French linens.

LA CUISINIERE
81–83 Northcote Road
London SW11
020 7223 4409
www.la.cuisiniere.co.uk
Kitchenware and jugs.

DAYLESFORD ORGANIC
www.daylesfordorganics.com
*Organic food and gorgeous home
accessories.*

DESIGN HOUSE STOCKHOLM
205 Kings Road
London SW3 5ED
www.designhousestockholm.com
Tabletop accessories.

DIBOR
www.dibor.co.uk
French bistro tableware.

FALKINERS
www.falkiners.com
*Decorative papers for runners,
coasters and mats.*

HABITAT
www.habitat.co.uk
Modern china, glass and cutlery.

HEAL'S
www.heals.co.uk
*Contemporary china, glassware,
cutlery, placemats and candles.*

IDYLLIC DAYS
www.idyllicdays.com
*Vintage china to hire for
weddings and parties.*

THE LACQUER CHEST
75 Kensington Church Street
London W8 4BG
020 7937 1306
www.lacquerchest.com
Decorative tableware and knick-knacks.

JOHN LEWIS
www.johnlewis.com
*Every type of tableware, from
the precious to the practical.*

LINUM IN IRELAND
www.linumireland.ie
Swedish table linens.

THE LITTLE THINGS
www.thelittlethings.co.uk
Place cards, tags and labels.

DAVID MELLOR DESIGN
4 Sloane Square
London SW1W 8EE
020 7730 4259
www.davidmellordesign.com
Beautifully designed cutlery.

NOT ON THE HIGH STREET
www.notonthehighstreet.com
Table linens, tags and tealight holders.

PARTY SUPERSTORE
268 Lavender Hill
London SW11 1LJ
020 7924 3210
www.partysuperstores.co.uk
Party plates, plastic glasses and cutlery.

THE PRINT GALLERY
www.theprintgallery.co.uk
Contemporary art for purchase.

SELFRIDGES
400 Oxford Street
London, W1A 1AB
020 8123 400
*Stylish tabletop accessories, fine
and casual dinner- and glassware.*

SKANDIUM
86 Marylebone High Street
London W1U 4QS
020 7935 2077
www.skandium.com
*Scandinavian modern cutlery,
china and glassware.*

THE TEA HOUSE
15a Neal Street
London WC2H 9PU
020 7240 7539
Fine teas and tea-making equipment.

VV ROULEAUX
54 Sloane Square
London SW1W 8AX
020 7730 3125
www.vvrouleaux.com
Ribbons and artificial flowers.

WARES OF KNUTSFORD
08456 121 273
www.waresofknutsford.co.uk
Enamel tableware.

WHIPPET
71 Bedford Hill
SW12 9HA
020 8772 9781
Gift boxes and cards.

ZARA HOME
129–131 Regent Street
London W1B 5SA
020 7432 0040
www.zarahome.com
*Gorgeous home accessories and a
particularly strong range of table linen.*

US SOURCES

ABC CARPET & HOME
888 & 881 Broadway
New York, NY 10003
212 473 3000
Visit www.abchome.com
for details of a retail outlet
near you.
*Handmade dinnerware, antique pieces,
and French terracotta tableware.*

JONATHAN ADLER
47 Greene Street
New York, NY 10013
212 941 8950
Visit www.jonathanadler.com
for details of their other stores.
*Groovy retro-modern serving dishes
and tabletop accessories.*

ANTHROPOLOGIE
Visit www.anthropologie.com
to find a store near you.
*Quirky, well-priced vintage-inspired
tableware and table linens.*

THE CONRAN SHOP
407 East 59th Street
New York, NY 10022
866 755 9079
www.conranusa.com
*Stylish tabletop accessories, fine
and casual china and glassware.*

CRATE & BARREL
Visit www.crateandbarrel.com
to find a store near you.
Stylish tableware at great prices.

DANSK
Visit www.dansk.com to find
a retailer near you.
*Scandinavian modern glassware,
flatware, and dinnerware.*

ENGLISH COUNTRY ANTIQUES
Snake Hollow Road
P. O. Box 1945
Bridgehampton, NY 11932
631 537 0606
*Period country furniture and
decorative accessories.*

FISHS EDDY
889 Broadway
New York, NY 10003
212 420 9020
Call 1 877 347 4733 or visit
www.fishseddy.com for their
other two store locations.
*Vintage-style dinnerware, flatware,
and glassware.*

GLOBAL TABLE
109 Sullivan Street
New York, NY 10012
212 431 5839
www.globaltable.com
*Exotic tableware, glassware, flatware,
sake sets, and unusual candles.*

GUMP'S
135 Post Street
San Francisco, CA 94108
800 766 7628
www.gumps.com
*Elegant and luxurious tabletop
accessories.*

IKEA
Call 800 434 IKEA or visit
www.ikea.com to find a store
near you.
*Cheap-and-cheerful tableware, decorative
serving platters, and table linen.*

MIKASA
www.mikasa.com
*Good-quality, reasonably priced
dinnerware, crystal, and flatware.*

MOSS
150 Greene Street
New York, NY 10012
866 888 6677
www.mossonline.com
Elegant dinnerware and flatware.

PIER ONE IMPORTS
Call 212 206 1911 or visit
www.pier1.com to find a store
near you.
*Seasonal selection of affordable,
trend-led vases.*

POTTERY BARN
Visit www.potterybarn.com
to find a store near you.
*Good-quality, good-value tabletop
items, whose eclectic good looks belie
the low prices.*

RUBY BEETS ANTIQUES
25 Washington Street
P.O. Box 1174
Sag Harbor, NY 11963
631 899 3275
www.rubybeets.com
*Holmegaard glass, Italian pewter
serving bowls and dishes, and Chinese
porcelain.*

TARGET STORES
Visit www.target.com to
find a store near you.
*Inexpensive china, flatware,
and tabletop accessories.*

THIBAUT
480 Frelinghuysen Avenue
Newark, NJ 07114
800 223 0704
www.thibautdesign.com
*Specialty wallpapers – perfect for
coasters and other decorative details.*

WILLIAM YEOWARD
Visit
www.williamyeowardcrystal.com
to find a retail outlet near you.
*Beautiful contemporary crystal from
this talented designer.*

index

picture credits

All photography by Debi Treloar except pages 133–139, which were photographed by David Brittain and styled by Emily Chalmers.

page 16 glassware from Design House Stockholm; page 17 decanter by Skandium, candlesticks from Ikea; page 19 cutlery/flatware in lined drawer, find similar at David Mellor; page 24 all vases and tealights, C. Best; page 30 three ceramic candleholders from Josephine Ryan Antiques; pages 34–35 plates and cutlery/flatware from Daylesford Organic; page 44 enamel plates and bowls from Wares of Knutford; page 48 vintage blanket from The Cloth Shop; page 53 turquoise enamel bucket from C. Best; page 53 tin containers from Ikea; page 58 china and cutlery/flatware from Brissi, glassware from Ceramica Blue; page 62 china and cutlery/flatware from Daylesford Organic; page 63 tags from Faulkiner's Fine Papers; page 68 glassware from Skandium and Design House Stockholm, decanter and black dinner plates from Skandium, candlesticks from Ikea; page 70 striped white plate from Design House Stockholm; page 71 Black retro glasses, stylist's own; page 72 candleholders from Josephine Ryan Antiques; ceramic cake plate, stylist's own; page 73 plates from David Mellor; tablecloth by The Cloth Shop; page 75 small cheeseboard from David Mellor, small wooden stars, The Print Gallery; page 85 Cutlery/flatware from David Mellor, napkin rings from Zara Home; page 88 antique tea set from Idyllic Days, cakes from Love Bakery London; page 116 glassware from David Mellor and Brissi; page 128 black placemats, tea block and small patterned teacups from The Tea House, Covent Garden.

business credits

Cupcakes on pages 88–93
supplied by:
Love Bakery London
319 Kings Road
London SW3 5EP
020 7352 3191
www.lovebakerylondon.com

Location on pages 62–67
and 112–115:
Sasha Waddell Fabrics & Furniture
at Teed Interiors Ltd.
020 8979 9189
www.sashawaddell.com

Flowers throughout by:
Flourish & Green
07957 364374
07764 938468
www.flourishandgreen.com

acknowledgments

My heartfelt thanks go to the fantastic team who have worked so hard to create this book. Their dedication and encouragement has led it to be such an exhilarating, inspiring and enjoyable experience.

Special thanks go to Leslie Harrington and her team who proposed the idea and gave me the opportunity to have my 'own book', of which I am so proud. To Jess for her patience and dedication in sourcing such great locations, to Megan for her elegant layouts and helpful support throughout, and, of course, to Rebecca, for bringing the visuals to life with her words. Thanks go to the shops that kindly loaned me props – this project would not be possible without them.

Last but not least, my thanks to Debi for capturing the atmosphere of each setting with her beautiful photographs, her endless ability to keep shooting, and her wonderful laughter. It's been an incredible journey with you all, thank you.

Liz Belton